CW00919426

BEVERLEY in Poems, Paintings and Prose

Peter Lee, Stephen Hill and Peter Hick

Printed in Yorkshire by Hart & Clough Ltd.

To Steve

Best Wishes and thanks for the beer !

Steve

Nab Wood Publications

1, Pasture Lane, Beverley, HU17 8DU
United Kingdom.

ISBN   978-1-9162300-0-2

© Peter Lee, Stephen Hill, Peter Hick 2019

The right of Peter Lee, Stephen Hill and Peter Hick to be identified as the authors of this work has been asserted by them in accordance with the Copyright, Designs and Patents Act 1988.

All rights reserved. No part of this publication may be reproduced, stored in a retrieval system or transmitted, in any form or by any means, electronic, mechanical, photocopying, recording, or otherwise, without the prior permission of Nab Wood Publications.

Printed and bound in Great Britain by Hart & Clough Ltd, Cleckheaton, BD19 4TQ.

Front cover: "Rooftops of Beverley". Human Design:www.humandesign.co.uk

PREFACE

THE REASON WHY

This is a volume of serendipity,
It isn't a guide, it isn't a history -
Its origins are wrapped in a mystery.

Perhaps it's a sort of State of the Nation
That's based upon old men's observation

Of a place they know well, a place that they love,
Where they've had good times, but heavens above…

…In a world that's plagued with doom and doubt
It's given them something to think about.

DEDICATION

TO BERYL, LOUISA, ROSEMARY AND ALL OUR BEVERLEY FRIENDS

FOREWORD

I am honoured to be Mayor of Beverley this year and as a result have been lucky enough to have had a preview of this new book about the town. I think the reflections by these three esteemed Beverlonians are a fine addition to what is already available on the subject. It puts a different slant on various people and places, is informative and pleasing to the eye. It has made me look at the town through different glasses and I am also pleased to say it made me chuckle!

Duncan Jack
Mayor of Beverley, 2019/20

ACKNOWLEDGEMENTS

The authors would like to express their appreciation to several people who were integral to the preparation of this book.
To Richard and Peter Clough and all their team at Hart & Clough who have produced a beautiful book, together with their generosity in supporting it. To Professor Barbara English for checking the historical information. To Chris Herman for hours of his time spent proof reading the notes and poems and Graham Scott of Human Design for the cover. To Dr David Bowden, Roger Shaw, Nel King and Mike and Tim at Richard White Advertising for their contributions. To Pamela Hopkins for allowing access to her writings, to the Beverley Civic Society and to all the authors and sources which we have listed at the end of the book. Thank you all.

PL, PH, SH. Beverley, August 2019.

HELP FOR HEALTH:
HELPING THE PEOPLE OF EAST YORKSHIRE and NORTH LINCOLNSHIRE.
A REGISTERED CHARITY SINCE 2002.

Formerly known as The Humberside Charitable Health Trust the charity was formed and registered in 2002 under the chairmanship of Roger King. In January of 2011, it was relaunched with a new name - "Help for Health" - and a new website. The Charity's mission statement is "Improving the health and well-being of people living in East Yorkshire and Northern Lincolnshire".

In seeking to achieve this aim the charity has, over the last decade and a half, awarded grants totalling in excess of two million pounds. Help for Health's financial assistance has supported local health related projects both big and small - from supporting major medical research to improving the health and lifestyles of individuals and groups. The charity, under the Chairmanship of Dr Andrew Milner, is controlled by a board of eight trustees with expertise in business, nursing, administration, accountancy, medicine and the law.

Please visit the website at www.helphealth.org.uk and obtain a more detailed account of the Charity's work, terms of funding and an on-line application form.

CONTENTS

NORTH BAR

Beverley has been surrounded by a barrier since mediaeval times. Initially this was an earth rampart and ditch with four entry/exit gates [called Bars] - namely North Bar, Norwood Bar, Keldgate [South] Bar and Newbegin Bar. Today, only North Bar remains. It was rebuilt in 1409 using locally sourced red clay bricks at a cost of £96.0s.11½d. The two storey structure has a room over the archway. On the north face there is a buttress on either side of the arch. Immediately above the apex of the arch is the carved stone coat of arms of the Warton family - who lived in the adjoining town [Bar]house. On the south face, above the arch, are three brick shields and recessed windows, all enclosed by a line of gablelike brickwork. In the olden days, the Bars were toll gates where traders paid for access. In his book 'Beverlac', George Poulson records North Bar as being the most lucrative - providing an income of £17.4s.8d in the year 1420! North Bar continues to be a feature of great importance to ceremonial Beverley. Closing and opening of the gates has taken place during re- enactments of medieval battles and in 2009, I remember, the gates were opened to admit the homecoming of the 1st Battalion of the Yorkshire Regiment.

NORTH BAR SOUTH FACE

PL
2019

2

NORTH BAR WITHIN

There's a North Bar Without and a North Bar Within.
Just two pubs Without, but dozens Within,
Which makes it a sensible place to begin.

There's the Standard, the Beaver, then turn left for Nellies
Where they've Tadcaster Ales and no bloody tellies,
And rooms lit by gas - yes that's what the smell is.

We've eaters from Turkey, Canton, Bangladesh.
From Italy, France and Thailand ...oh yes
If you want something English try Pizza Express

We have fashion and footwear and hairdressers too.
A cafe for cyclists, and Murray Todd who
Looks after the Gents who appear in Who's Who.

Just a few of the attractions in the Georgian Quarter
And should you, dear friend, spend more than you oughta,
We've a real live Bank which is there to support ya.

NORTH BAR - NORTH FACE

R. 2019

4

THE ROYAL STANDARD INN

On the east side of North Bar Within, the striking black and white frontage and beautiful hanging baskets of the Royal Standard are a familiar and welcoming sight for many locals. The building was originally timber framed but was converted to a rendered front in the 1850s. The 'dram shop' window was added in the 1870s and remains today, albeit with different glass. The first drinking establishment at this site was called The Boot [1851], subsequently becoming The Turf Inn [1858] and finally The Royal Standard in the 1870s.

For three generations the Wild family were landlords starting with Thomas Charles Winson, then George Wild and finally Kenneth Arthur Wild. At one time the back bar was known as Dolly's Bar, where Dolly Wild presided for 34 years. When Ken and Joyce retired the Wild family had been landlords of The Standard for 100 years! Thanks to the presence of its 'rich' and varied habitués from all walks of life, the front bar remains a haven of conversation and repartee – long may it continue.

THE ROYAL STANDARD

The famed Royal Standard on North Bar Within
Was always the pub I used to drink in.
For at least thirty years and possibly more
I've been going through its open front door.

In the earlier days, when Ken was the host
The bar at the front was my usual post.
And many a pint was memorably sunk
With my lawyer friend Les, though we never got drunk.

There was Acker and Dange, Dave, Jim and Kenny
Ewan and Bruce and others there were many.
There are some no longer with us, but it's good to know
That the fun and the laughter is still in full flow.

I have to confess now I don't go as much,
But the bar at the back sometimes keeps me in touch.
And I think of old friends and the good times we had
And I smile and remember and the memories are glad.

8

THE BEVERLEY ARMS HOTEL

Records suggest that an Inn known as 'The Bell' existed in Beverley in 1686 and this was probably 'The Blue Bell Inn'. In 1794 adjacent premises were added and the Inn was renamed 'The Beverley Arms'. This major refurbishment was carried out by a local builder called William Middleton. In the 1850s the property was acquired by the Morley family and served as a 'Posting Inn', where horses could be changed during long journeys. In 1938 the property was acquired by Trust House Ltd and in 1970 became part of the Trust House Forte Group. Despite being a Grade 2 listed building, an extensive refurbishment was carried out in 1966/7. The original property was altered beyond recognition with construction of the hideous five storey 'white' extension, which was until very recently a notorious 'blot' on the Beverley landscape.

The hotel fell into administration in 2016 and was acquired by the Lancashire based company Daniel Thwaites. The architects Bowman Riley supervised a sympathetic rebuild and refurbishment, with demolition of the five storey block and single storey extension and conservatory at the rear. The work was finished in July 2018, and at a preview evening to mark the reopening of the Hotel a time capsule was buried by local businessman Mr. Andrew Marr, aided by the CEO of Thwaites Mr. Richard Bailey. All could now see that Beverley had, once more, an historic hotel of which it could be proud.

But what of the folklore of the hotel? Well, it is said that Dick Turpin stayed there in 1738 when he appeared before the town magistrates. Some will tell you that a ghost was present when the older sections of the hotel existed. Anthony Trollope was based at the hotel when he stood as Parliamentary candidate for Beverley in 1868. My own favourite link with the hotel's past is the oil paintings by famed local artist Fred Elwell, depicting so beautifully the hotel kitchen in bygone days. You don't even need to visit the art gallery - just walk past the hotel and see the reproductions of 'Three Maids' and 'Preparations' hanging there on the archway wall.

THE BEVERLEY ARMS

This fine old Hotel it was in dire straits,
Abandoned, forlorn and left to the fates.
No saviour it seemed would appear at the gates,
When out of the blue came some brewers called Thwaites.

Well over the Pennines they actually came
With a long pedigree and a very good name.
And it soon became clear they're on top of the game
And the Beverley Arms is back in the frame.

We knew that the guys were on the right track
When they knocked down that horrible block at the back
In a well executed full frontal attack,
And we gave them a mental pat on the back.

St MARY'S CHURCH

Construction of this magnificent Parish Church began may have begun in the 12th century when Thurstan, Archbishop of York, began to develop the north end of Beverley, although the church is not mentioned in any documents until 1269. All through the middle ages it was a parochial chapel dependent on the Minster. The original building consisted of a simple nave, tower and chancel. However over the next 400 years, a constant programme of alterations and additions resulted in the Church we see today. Important added features were the vaulted crypt (originally a charnel or bone house), the exquisitely constructed St Michael's Chapel, the Priest's room over this chapel and the uniquely decorated chancel ceiling with its 40 panels depicting British Monarchs.

Such were the extent of the building works that in 1520, during a Sunday service, a total collapse of the tower and a significant part of the nave occurred, with the loss of 55 lives. Repairs and rebuilding were rapidly instigated but no more major building works were carried out.

St Mary's is visited and admired by many visitors every year. Often their interest is focused on two very different features of the Church - the "White Rabbit" and the "Bullet Hole". These may represent the extremes of the Church's long history!

The White Rabbit is a small curved figure of a "Pilgrim Rabbit" dating from about 1335, which may have been known to Lewis Carroll author of Alice in Wonderland. Some say it was the inspiration for the White Rabbit illustrations. The bullet hole resulted from a machine gun bullet fired from a German plane during the Second World War. The bullet entered the Church through a window on the south side of the nave and went through the back of a pew. Yes, in the third pew up from the West door you can still see and put your finger in the bullet hole!

14

ST MARY'S

The Minster stands alone and grand.
St Mary's, on the other hand,
For different purposes was planned.

A Parish Church to serve the town,
A place of worship of their own.
The House of God, hand built in stone.

Standing at the heart of things
A sort of reverence it brings.
The bells ring out. The choir sings.

Across the road, the Beverley Arms,
Is now restored to former charms.
Both welcome us with open arms.

Nine centuries, the Church has stood,
In the bad times and the good.
Just as the founders hoped it would.

Enter through the great West Door.
Think you've seen it once before?
King's College Chapel and what's more
Ours was built long years before.

Take a wander down the aisles.
Admire the architectural styles,
From Early English in particular
To what's known as Perpendicular.

Go in the Chancel, it's unique ceiling,
Has forty portraits each revealing,
One of our Monarchs, who reigned betwixt
The mythic Brutus and Henry Six

There were disasters on the way.
The Black Death caused a long delay
As artisans were swept away.

And then, what congregations dread,
The Tower collapsed, with many dead
And many more it has been said....

...Would have died were it not for
Bear Baiting taking place next door.
The moral being? Not too sure.

Now Pevsner says, in his researches
Of all the English Parish Churches,
St Mary's is amongst the best.
That says it all. Our case we rest.

THE WHITE HORSE INN [NELLIE'S]

A hostelry has stood on this site from before 1666. Originally a coaching inn called the White Horse Hotel, today it is called the White Horse Inn [or Nellie's] but still retains the interior of a 19th century pub. There are narrow, dark passages with uneven stone and wooden floors. Multiple little rooms lit by gas light, filled with bric-a-brac, ancient tables and chairs and in the main bar a roaring fire and rickety lumpy benches.

The Collinsons who owned the pub from 1927 are long gone now, but locals will still tell you of the three daughters [Nellie, Ada and Dorothy] who served the beer from hand pumps set on a table beside two bowls of water used to wash and rinse the glasses. Pamela Eldred's account of Nellie Collinson is featured in Barbara English's Extraordinary Women of Beverley - well worth a look.

Since 1975, the pub has been owned by Samuel Smiths Brewery. Thankfully, despite several attempts to alter the interior, it remains today as a unique environment for drinking, guarded over by the White Horse – now made of fibreglass but for a long time the wooden rocking horse of one Richard [Dicky] Whiting, or so the late Pat Deans tells us!

Nellies

18

NELLIE'S

The White Horse? He asked
As I walked down the street,
Just a minute, I said
As I thought on my feet.

Oh, Nellie's you'll mean,
I managed to say,
Just two hundred yards
Down that a'way.

Dark, damp and dim
That's how you'll find it,
As it always has been
Though nobody minds it.

But no longer the jug
Or the washing up bowl,
No more dear Nellie
Who gave the place soul.

But the spirit lives on
A time warp its frame,
Whilst the fire crackles slowly
You'll be glad that you came.

SATURDAY MARKET and THE MARKET CROSS

In the 12th Century a new market was built in the north of the town. By the 16th century it had become known as Saturday Market. At various sites within the market, and at differing times, sections selling corn, fish, meat, butter and poultry were developed. In 1886 the Corn Market was moved to a large red brick building – still present to this day – subsequently being occupied by the Picture Playhouse Cinema and today by Browns Shop. A market day has taken place on nearly every Saturday since the market's inception - even through the Great War years. Today, up to 120 stall holders sell their wares - coming from as far away as Manchester, Nottingham and Lincolnshire. In recent years the Christmas Market held on a Sunday in December has become an 'institution'. It is said that many thousands of people visited the Christmas Market in 2018. Equally popular, the Beverley Food Festival takes place on a Saturday in November, with folk flocking to taste delicious local products and produce as well as an eclectic mix of foreign delicacies.

A cross was erected in the market in the 15th Century but it was demolished and the current Market Cross was built between 1711 and 1714. The cross was designed by the architect Samuel Shelton of Wakefield. The shelter is square with canted corners; it has eight Roman Doric columns supporting the roof on which there is a cupola surmounted by a lantern, an obelisk and a weather vane. Eight limestone vases were added in 1797. The cross bears the Beverley Borough Arms and the heraldic arms of Queen Anne, Sir Charles Hotham and Sir Michael Warton. The latter two were Members of Parliament for the town and provided some of the finance for the Cross. On the south side, above the coats of arms is a cartouche (tablet) carved with trophies of arms (displays of weaponry and other militaria to signify victory or military power) and a head with a headdress of feathers. The brass plate in the centre of this cartouche is inscribed as follows:

"This cross was built at the expense of Sr. Charles Hotham Bart. and Sr. Michael Warton Kt.
Members of Parliament for Anno Domini 1714. Repaired in Ao 1769 Wm. Leake Esq.Mayor."

Always the centre of the market activity, the Cross looks particularly attractive at Christmas with a decorated tree and floodlighting.

22

SATURDAY MARKET

If the Westwood's the lungs, and the Minster the mind,
It is here where perhaps the town's heart you'll find.

It was here that the villagers came in to trade
The things that they'd grown and the garments they'd made,
The poultry they'd reared and the eggs what they'd laid.

After nine hundred years the Market survives.
It is a big part of the towns peoples lives
And generally speaking the Market place thrives.

For liquid refreshment, there are the King's Head,
The Green Dragon, the Windmill and it has to be said,
They're enough Coffee Shops, if you want that instead.

There are wonderful shops, yes truly there are.
And shoppers they know this, they come from afar,
Though finding a place to park the damned car....

THE MARKET CROSS

A Market Cross is the focal point,
Of any respectable Georgian Town.
And ours is a truly handsome one
As befits our handsome Town.

But what is so lucky about our Cross,
And remarkable in this sense is,
It was funded by our two MP's

Did they put it down to expenses?

WEDNESDAY MARKET

A market place has been present on this site since the 12th century. Originally known as Southern Market, it was renamed Fish Market and in 1446 became Wednesday Market. In the 18th century it was sometimes referred to as Cockpit or Cockpit Hill because the market was used for cockfights. A cross was probably built in the market in 1723 by Henry Jarrett but was pulled down in 1730 /31, when it was described as a cockpit of timber and tiles known as 'Wednesday Market Cross'. It was then rebuilt incorporating stone by John Rushworth. In 1762/3 it was again rebuilt, this time in the form of an obelisk [British History on line] but removed in 1881. The market place has been altered many times - most recently in 1846 for the construction of Railway Street, and in 1909 for Lord Roberts Road.

Trading ceased in Wednesday Market in the mid 18th century when Saturday Market became dominant, but market days on both Wednesday and Saturday recommenced in 1997.

The shops of Wednesday Market have been home to several family businesses much beloved by the towns' residents – namely Jack's Delicatessen, Ye Olde Pork Shoppe and Peck's Fishmongers. Not so much loved was Crystal's Garage, which was built on the site of the old Methodist chapel in 1958, remaining there until 1997 until replaced by Boyes Shop - the only 20th century building in the Market Place.

An alehouse has probably stood on the north side of the market since the 16thcentury, with evidence that it was certainly known as The Queen's Head in 1802. The original building was of plain red brick, later stuccoed, but was converted to its now familiar black and white [mock Tudor] frontage by Darley's Brewery in 1926.

Wednesday Markets
2013 PL

WEDNESDAY MARKET

Leave the car if you can park it,
Take a stroll around this market.

See Mr Peck who sells fresh fish
He'll find you anything you wish,
Not overpriced, not overrated,
Not clingfilm wrapped , not sell by dated.

Mr. Jack's who were next door
In fact they had been since the war,
Have taken to a well earned rest
But are remembered as the best.

Across the square you should stop
And look into Ye Olde Pork Shoppe,
Though 'tis not ours to reason why
A pork shop may not sell pork pie.

Now one of modern life's great joys is
To go and shop at dear old Boyeses.
If you can't find it, bet they'll have it,
For they seem to have a habit
Of knowing precisely what is needed,
And how well they have succeeded.

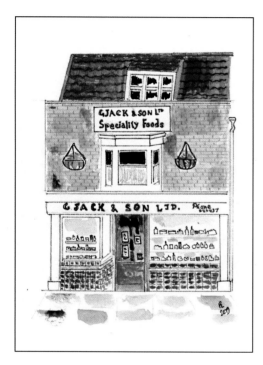

Jack's Speciality Foods

Ye Olde Pork Shoppe

Peck's Fishmongers

WEDNESDAY MARKET SHOPS

George Jack and Son

George Jack and Son began trading in Wednesday Market in 1961, when the business was managed by George's son, David. Prior to this the Care/Jack family had been involved with groceries and retail groceries in Beverley for a hundred years, having had premises in both Saturday Market and Eastgate. In 1995 David's son Duncan joined the business and he and his wife Joy ran the shop until 2015. Famous for the lovely pork pies baked in their Flemingate bakery, Jack's always had a large cohort of faithful customers. When Joy and Duncan retired, the business was renamed 'Adeli'. In March 2019 the business changed hands again and, with a new coat of dark green paint and a smart green and white awning, has now become a fruit and vegetable shop.

Ye Olde Pork Shoppe

This unique butchers shop, probably present at this site from the mid 19th century, also doubled up as a pub - The Spotted Cow - one of four taverns in Wednesday Market at that time. There cannot have been many places where you could have a pint while your meat was butchered! The shop was run for many years by the Hillman family. It ceased to offer its pub facilities around 1937, but has remained as a butchers ever since. Now run by Peter Brinham, the building still has the trapdoor to the old beer cellar under the front counter, the hundred year old smoker through the back and even an original outside 'loo' [which still works!].

H.Peck and Son, Fish Monger

Harold and Jessie Peck opened the family fish monger business in 1939 and it has been at number 7 ever since. Very soon Harold went off to war, so that the task of running the shop fell to 'Grandma' – says Josie, who presently runs the family business with Alan and Mark. In the early days the family lived above the shop, and the internal structure of the 18th century listed building remains almost unchanged. The shop is always spick and span both outside and in. When Hull was still a thriving fishing port the fish would come fresh from the docks. Now it mostly comes pre frozen from Norway and Iceland - but still tastes the best!

HIGHGATE

The road running south from Beverley's 'Southern Market Place' [or Fishmarket] probably existed in the 12th century and it became known as Highgate in the 15th century. Highgate is similar to High Street although the Viking influence in Beverley has led to the incorporation of the Danish word for 'street' - gata - into several road names [Lairgate, Hengate, Highgate]. The road's importance as the main access from the town to the Minster was exemplified by the construction of the elaborate North Porch of the Minster in 14/15th century.

In the 18th century Highgate was known as 'Londoners Street' because many of the buildings were occupied by London Merchants who came for the nine day Cross Fair held on Highgate. By the mid 18th century most of these shops had been replaced by houses. Mention should be made of the Monk's Walk Tavern at number 19, which was originally called The Old George or The George and Dragon. The original buildings were probably two timber cottages separated by a passageway – which still exists. Behind its 18th century facade there is a 17th century fragment dated 1671 and in other areas the mediaeval timbers remain.

Further down on the opposite side, across a lawn, at right angles to the site of the Blue Coats School is the new [1963] Minster Vicarage which replaced the 'Old Vicarage' in Minster yard. In 1968, Highgate was declared a conservation area. In 1990, W. Stephenson observed the results of a trench dug across Highgate for drainage. The average depth of the trench was 2.1m. The substratum was a black peaty material, with hazel branches on top, and then trunks of young trees, above which were large irregular blocks of chalk and other stones. Finally, the street has been raised to its modern level by a thick layer of soil, clay and smaller stones with the granite setts on top. Walking down it will never feel the same again!

Highgate

34

HIGHGATE

Turn into Highgate ancient street,
Where for centuries ill shod feet
Trod the Market – Minster beat
On Saxon loam and compressed peat.

Observe the Highgate nowadays
Where modern tourists stop and gaze,
To marvel, and indeed to praise
The glories of our yesterdays.

EAST RIDING THEATRE (THE FORMER BAPTIST CHAPEL)

The "Art Nouveau Gothic" style red brick and stone building on Lord Roberts Road was, for a long time, the Baptist Chapel. It was constructed in 1910 to replace the Well Lane Chapel which was demolished when Lord Roberts Road was constructed. The building was a gift from Admiral Charles Walker to the Particular Baptists of Beverley, and was designed by GF Pennington of the West Riding Architects Garside and Pennington. Until its closure in 1964 it remained a place of Baptist worship for 54 years. Owned by the East Riding of Yorkshire, from 2000 until 2007, it was occupied by the East Riding Archive.

Beverley has a long tradition of theatre and culture, going back to the mystery plays performed in the open air during the Middle Ages at stations across the town, including North Bar, the Fish market (now Wednesday Market) and Cross Bridge. The first purpose built theatre in Beverley was in Walkergate and subsequently in Cross Street and then Lairgate on the corner of Champney Road. The theatre in Lairgate closed in 1840. Although a number of buildings were used for performances, Beverley has remained without a dedicated theatre until very recently.

In 2012 the actor Vincent Regan, a local resident, instituted the rejuvenation of Beverley's theatre life. Together with Sue Kirkman he set up 'East Riding Theatre Company Ltd'. In March 2013 they were granted a peppercorn lease by ERYC to occupy the former Baptist Chapel. The lease was dependent on renovation. With the massive and untiring support and enthusiasm of local volunteers, including craftsmen, tradesmen and businesses, the transformation of the former chapel into a theatre of which everyone could be proud was completed. A one night trial opening event 'An Evening with Barrie Rutter' took place on 12th December 2014, and to rapturous applause and enormous praise the first in house production (Dickens's 'A Christmas Carol') took place on December 17th, 2014.

Since then the theatre has continued to thrive, not only with West End calibre plays but also with music, comedy and, most importantly, a convivial café–bar. The high standards of the ERT productions have brought immense joy to the East Yorkshire folk and beyond. Now the hard work of the volunteers, actors, producers, technicians and administrative staff is being recognised further afield – exemplified by the comments in the Times newspaper series 'Best Places to Live in UK, 2019'. Thank you ERT for bringing so much pleasure into our lives.

THE EAST RIDING THEATRE

Our town is more than shops and pubs
And restaurants and sporting clubs,
Although they play a crucial role
Promoting Beverley as a whole.

And are we not well catered for?
Cultural activities galore -
Music, cinema and the arts
They all play important parts.

But what we needed in our town
Was a theatre of our own.
We all agreed no doubt about it,
But just hang on, just think about it.

Imagine what they had to do,
That Vincent Regan, Tom and Sue.
All those hoops to be jumped through -
To sum it up in one word, Phew!

With massive help from volunteers
And lots of sweat and lots of tears,
The place was opened in two years
To resounding heartfelt cheers.

I was expecting Beverley
But when before my eyes
I saw the Minster hanging there
Against the Summer Skies
It filled me with astonishment
With wonder and surprise

I cannot help but thinking
Wherever that I go
It's not the modern material things
That stop and move me so
But Churches and Cathedrals built
Many hundreds of years ago.

After J.B. Priestley in English Journey, 1934

BEVERLEY MINSTER

In the 8th century John, the Bishop of Hexham and later Bishop of York, retired and founded a monastery at Inderawuda, which is traditionally regarded as the site upon which the Minster now stands. The first church was probably built of timber. John's reputation grew because of the healing miracles he performed. He died in 721 and is buried in the church he founded. In 1037, Bishop John was canonised. The site was visited by great numbers of pilgrims in the 12th century and later and became one of the most famous places in the country. King Edward 1st borrowed the banner of St John and bestowed generous gifts on the Minster. Later the cult of St John received a further boost when Henry V won the battle of Agincourt on one of St John's feast days and made John one of the patron saints of the Royal Family.

The church was rebuilt in the new Norman style between the 1060s and 70s, but in 1188 a fire badly damaged the church and in about 1213 the tower collapsed. During subsequent years the rebuilding continued, changing in building style as architectural fashion dictated. There are now distinct sections showing the Early English style, the Decorated style and the Perpendicular style which was in favour when the building was completed in 1420. Since then other restorations have been completed and the Minster is in good repair and is regarded by many as the finest medieval church in Europe.

The Minster is 393 feet long with two West towers, a long nave, twin transepts, quire, sanctuary and a retroquire. It is primarily a place of worship; if you are able, attend a service - unforgettable with the towering acoustics in historic surroundings. Otherwise, make sure to see the sanctuary chair, the Percy Canopy, the misericord (mercy) seats in the quire, the tomb of St. John and the medieval musician carvings as well as the font and the statues of St John and King Athelstan.

There are many 'secrets' in the Minster. Above the crossing in the roof is the tread wheel. This human hamster wheel is used to raise a decorated roof boss so that building materials can be hoisted into the central tower. Glaziers have engraved pictures of all the different types of planes which have been in service at RAF Leconfield on the north transept rose window, along with the names of former church wardens.

Many of the 6,000 visitors to the Minster each year ask two questions – what is the difference between a minster and a cathedral, and where are the toilets! A minster (Latin: Monasterium) is an early church where a community of priests lived and worked as missionaries in the surrounding area. In 1548 Beverley Minster became, and remains, a parish church. A cathedral is where the diocesan bishop has his seat (Latin: Cathedra). Our Minster's cathedral is York Minster.

42

THE MINSTER

In seven hundred and twenty one
Occurred the death of Bishop John,
Whereby a legend was begun.

He was a saintly man indeed
According to the Venerable Bede,
And in due course the Pope agreed.

A shrine was built and pilgrims came
And Beverley became a name,
For Bishop John had brought it fame.

The miracles St John had wrought
Came to the ears of men at Court,
So 'ere a battle could be fought….

…Kings must board the East Coast Line
To say a prayer at St John's shrine,
The outcome always turned out fine.

And Kings victorious in the field
Who'd forced the Scots or French to yield,
A generous nature was now revealed.

And so the Church's coffers grew
For Royals contributed too,
And Church and Town were well to do.

But then disaster struck, alas
As canons were attending Mass,
Stones started falling from the Tower.
It was the Church's darkest hour.

The Tower collapsed, the building crumbled,
The Clergy they were shaken, humbled.
The stolid Beverlonians grumbled.

What happened next is quite amazing.
An act of faith and fundraising,
Quite inspired, truly trailblazing.

A building of outstanding grace.
A stunning yet a holy place,
Beverley's world famous face.

BEVERLEY BECK AND BECKSIDE

The Beck is a short canal of 0.8 miles that runs from Grovehill Lock on the River Hull into Beverley.

It seems likely that Beverley Beck was created in the 12th century when Archbishop Thurstan encouraged the townsfolk to deepen the Flemingate branch of Waterbeck, the natural stream that ran down from Westwood. In 1296 the Archbishop of York negotiated for the fish weirs to be removed from the River Hull. In this way the link from Beverley to the River Hull and thence to the Humber was created – a hugely important step in the commercial development of Beverley. Goods were imported to Beverley from Europe and exported from the developing industrial towns of West Yorkshire. Grovehill (Grevale) staith near the junction of the beck and river Hull was used as a mooring place for the barges, and the ship and boat building industries alongside the beck were able to develop and prosper. Amongst other industries that developed were the tanning industry, tile and brick making, milling and brewing.

Two Acts of Parliament were passed in 1727 which legalised a duty to be charged on all goods shipped or landed. The money was for cleaning, deepening, widening and repairs. Until 1802 the beck was tidal, but in that year the Grovehill Lock was built and the Beverley and Barmston Drain constructed to accommodate it.

In 1882 the first iron ships were built at Grovehill by Henry and Joseph Scarr. The shipbuilding firm of Cook, Welton and Gemmell Ltd. took over the site in 1902, mainly building trawlers for the Hull ocean going fleet. The shipyards finally closed in 1977, but there are still many Beverlonians who will recount to you their childhood memories of the pomp and ceremony of the ship launchings. Because of the width of the waterway the ships were, most unusually, launched sideways and taken down the River Hull to Princes Dock shipyard for fitting out.

Commercial traffic on the canal gradually diminished over the years – probably because of competition firstly from Hull, then from the railways and the increasing size of barges but was still taking place into the 1970's. A major refurbishment of the Beck and Beckside, started in 2005, has enhanced its survival as a place to live, to cycle, fish and walk. It is an accessible waterway for boats and boating and a home to the former Hodgsons Tannery barge the Syntan, beautifully restored by the Beverley Barge Preservation Society. And if that's not enough, don't forget to look at the statue of the Creeler at the Beck Head – part of the 39 pieces of art of The Beverley Town Trail, and my favourite.

BECKSIDE

In eighteen hundred was devised
A forward looking enterprise.
The Beck was tamed and canalised,
A lock gate built and organised.

Now famous Tanners tanned their hide,
Now ships were built with skill and pride.
And as the River wasn't wide,
The laws of logic were defied
And Trawlers launched upon their side.

BEVERLEY WESTWOOD HOSPITAL

(Formerly Beverley Base, Beverley Public Assistance Institution and Beverley Union Workhouse).

The original red brick Tudor style building, the centre piece of the Westwood Hospital site, was designed by the York architects John and William Atkinson and built in 1860/1861 as the Beverley Union Workhouse. In 1892/4, a sixty bed Infirmary was added, and in 1895 a new arched entrance complete with keystone and scrolls was erected and stood largely unchanged until 2016. The workhouse subsequently became the Beverley Public Assistance Institution. In 1939, with the advent of war, it became Beverley Base Hospital. In 1940, eight timber built wards were added. In 1948, with war over, it became the much loved Beverley Westwood Hospital. The timber built wards opening onto a single long corridor with two operating theatres in the centre provided general medical, surgical and orthopaedic care, with many hundreds of cases being operated upon each year. Similarly the Maternity unit provided obstetric facilities for the surrounding area. A new Obstetric Unit was opened in 1988 by Princess Diana in a stunning bright red dress.

Sadly (and controversially) the powers that be decided to move many of the facilities to Hull Royal and Castle Hill Hospitals. Although the buildings continued to function as the Beverley Community Hospital, many of them fell into disrepair (including the almost new Obstetric Building) and the hospital ceased to exist in 2012. The hugely valuable land has subsequently been developed as a housing estate. Some of the historic buildings have retained their 'original' external structure (the central Red Brick Building known as West House, Beaver Lodge and the Masters Board Room) but, sadly, one is no longer permitted to walk the time honoured pathway through the grounds.

50

AN ODE TO WESTWOOD HOSPITAL

Some called it Beverley Westwood,
The Oldies, Beverley Base.
Before that it was the Workhouse,
Quite a foreboding place.

Eight Nissen huts they built for war,
And these remained on site.
Our much loved local hospital
Helped many in their plight.

Medicine, Surgery, O and G,
Outpatients, physio and even A and E.
Two operating theatres, busy too,
Tending for the needs of me and you.

Then someone in the NHS
Decided Swinemoor would be the best.
Centralisation and access they say,
And so the hospital moved away.

Now we have smart houses there,
Perhaps a cause of some despair.
They call it progress, yes indeed,
I'm not so sure, am I naïve?

WESTWOOD AND THE PASTURE OF HURN
(Westwood with Hurn, Westwood Pasture or Westwood Common)

Westwood (with Hurn), at about 600 acres, is the biggest of Beverley's three commons - the others are Figham and Swinemoor. The present boundaries differ little from those shown in the Ordnance Survey of 1852. The common is roughly a square with Hurn View, Burton Bushes, the Imrey's Whiting Works and the Grammar School at its corners (perhaps not wholly archeologically correct but understandable!). It is traversed by several roads: York Road to the north, Newbald Road in the middle and Westwood Road and Walkington Road in the south.

The first mention of Westwood was in the 13th century when it was recorded as a woodland. In the mid 13th century, Simon de Bovill, the Archbishop of York, agreed 'common' rights for the Westwood and in 1379 Archbishop Nevill granted the land to the townsmen of Beverley. The 1836 Beverley Pasture Act confirmed the right of the freemen of Beverley to elect twelve Pasture Masters to govern Westwood, but a successful appeal meant that Beverley Corporation still owned the land. When common land had to be registered in 1977, the Land Commission confirmed the 1836 amendment – meaning, bizarrely, that East Riding of Yorkshire Council owns the soil but the Pasture Masters the grass!

So what features of the dim and distant past can we view on Westwood? Well, there are several Bronze Age and Iron Age Burial mounds, and at least two earthwork enclosures which may or may not have been Romano British defended settlements. Newbegin pits (where we sledge in winter) were the site of clay extraction from the middle ages and also the site of bull baiting (banned in 1824]. The area of the Lime Kiln pits can be seen to the south of Newbald Road and Valley.

Of the five Windmills originally on Westwood only two remain – the Black Mill and the Anti Mill which is now part of the golf clubhouse. Westwood was used in the First World War as a landing strip and troop encampment, and in the Second World War was cultivated to produce vegetables. Little evidence of this involvement remains, although a spigot mortar base near Newbegin Pits and some anti glider pillars can still be seen.

Today, Westwood remains as a source of income to the Pasture Masters from cattle and sheep grazing, the golf course and the race course, but more importantly it stands as a place of beauty and leisure for the people of Beverley. Cock fighting and bull baiting have all 'amused' in the past. Racing has taken place on Westwood for centuries - perhaps originally on 'The Tan', the track around the Blackmill so called because it was lined with bark from the Beverley Tanneries - and then on the 'formal' racecourse on the Hurn. Golf has been played on the Westwood course since before 1889. Today, usually in great harmony, hikers, dog walkers, runners, footballers, picnickers, hangliders and model plane and car enthusiasts flock to take advantage of its open spaces, protected from the sometime self interest of government agencies, planners and developers. Long may it continue.

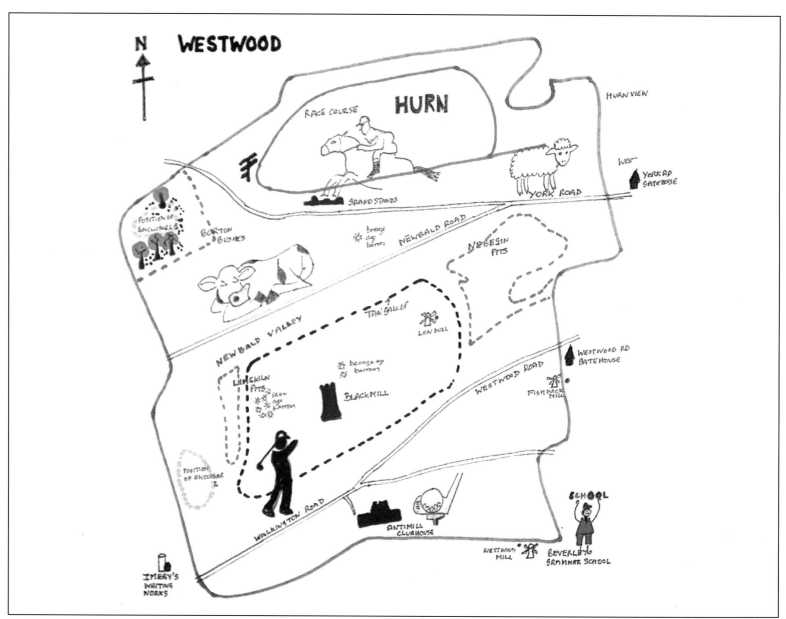

WESTWOOD

N

HURN

RACE COURSE

GRAND STANDS

POSITION OF ENCLOSURE 6

BURTON BUSHES

bronze age barrow

NEWBALD ROAD

NEBESIN PITS

YORK ROAD

HURN VIEW

WEST YORK RD GATEHOUSE

NEWBALD VALLEY

TAN GALLOP

LOW MILL

bronze age barrows

LIMEKILN PITS

IRON AGE barrow

BLACK MILL

WESTWOOD ROAD

WESTWOOD RD GATEHOUSE

FISHWICK MILL

POSITION OF ENCLOSURE 2

WALKINGTON ROAD

ANTIMILL CLUBHOUSE

SCHOOL

WESTWOOD MILL

BEVERLEY GRAMMER SCHOOL

IMERY'S WHITING WORKS

LIFE ON THE WESTWOOD

There is life on the Westwood, the lungs of the town,
It is one of the treasures that's been handed down,
A part of the reason for Beverley's renown.

There are dogs on the Westwood, they're out there each day,
Their owners it seems do not have much to say,
For Beverley dogs tend to get their own way.

There are cows on the Westwood for much of the year,
They keep the grass short and they've no sense of fear
As their road etiquette makes abundantly clear.

There are cyclists and runners and joggers as well,
How much they enjoy it is quite hard to tell
But one has the feeling they're going through hell.

They've played golf on the Westwood for a century or more.
They've had some good golfers, that is to be sure,
But the cattle don't heed when a golfer shout fore.

There are thousands of people who come for the races
For a right good day out, there are few better places,
You can pick out the winners by the look on their faces.

Here, the Holderness Hunt holds its Boxing Day meet
For a horse friendly town an equestrian treat,
And a blessing for those who've had too much to eat.

On the fifth of November there's a firework display
And a bonfire so bright it turns night into day,
And all of the profits go Charity's Way.

In winter there's sledging whenever there's snow.
When there's no parking spaces that's where the cars go,
And hope that the Pasture Masters don't know.

56

WESTWOOD MILLS

The Ordanance Survey map of 1852 showed there were five corn mills on or adjoining the Westwood.

Today there are partial remains of only three of them.

In 1852 the mills were:

1. **Westwood Hither Mill** (Low Mill, Crathorne's Mill or Wilson's Mill) which stood between Black Mill and the south west corner of Newbegin Pits. The mill was probably built in 1646, subsequently blown down in 1715 and rebuilt in 1742. It was demolished on the instructions of the Pasture Masters around 1854.

2. **Union Mill** (Anti Mill) which stood at the south west corner of the Westwood. The Union Mill Society was established in 1799 as a cooperative for farmers to mill their own grain, but a breakaway movement occurred and hence the name Anti Mill. In the 1890s it fell into disuse. The upper part was dismantled but the tower still remains as part of the golf course clubhouse.

3. **Fishwick Mill** (Butt Close Mill) A 'post' type mill, it stood on the eastern boundary of the Westwood near St Giles Croft. It was burned down in 1861 during the Fishwick Mill Riot - a public disturbance which took place over disputed rights of ownership between the Corporation and the Pasture Masters. The hump on which the Mill stood is now called Duffil's Mound and is all that is left to be seen of the mill and site.

4. **Westwood Mill** (Lowson's Mill, Jakeman's Mill) was in a close, adjacent to the Westwood near where the Grammar School now stands. It was a brick tower mill with five sails but was dismantled in 1891. The lower part of the tower still remains.

Lastly, although not chronologically so, the Black Mill is worthy of a little more detail because it remains as the distinctive landmark of present day Westwood.

5. **Westwood Far Mill (**Baitson's Mill, Cricketer's Mill, the **Black Mill**). First mentioned in 1654 it was initially a 'post' type corn mill, only later becoming wind powered. The mill was rebuilt in 1803 by Joseph Baitson. Following a fire in 1868, the working gear was removed by the Pasture Masters but the Mill House and tower remained. The land around was then used for cricket and football. In 1891 a pavilion was built in the garden of the Mill House which was then occupied by Mr and Mrs John Smith. It served as the clubhouse for the newly formed golf club with the Smiths acting as caretakers and caterers. In 1906 the pavilion was dismantled and moved to the golf course's new clubhouse on the Anti Mill site. Disuse and time took their toll on the tower, but after refurbishment in 2002/3 and again in 2019 the iconic landmark continues to dominate Westwood from every angle.

58

WESTWOOD MILLS

There were five mills on Westwood/ Hurn,
Paddles they did slowly turn,
Grinding corn both night and day
But now they've mostly gone away.

Low Mill, Far Mill, Union or Black
Crathorne, Fishwick. Butt's Close and that's
Not all, Baitson's, Cricketers, Jakeman and more,
So many to choose from, names galore.

So go for a walk on the 'hallowed' ground,
See what remnants can be found.
And if you can, prolong your stay
To catch Black Mill at close of day.

BEVERLEY AND EAST RIDING GOLF CLUB

The inaugural meeting of the Beverley and East Riding Golf Club was held at the Holderness Hotel, Beverley on 23rd October 1889. It seems likely that the 9 holes of the Club, centered on the Black Mill, had been in use for some years before that. The Club used the buildings around the Black Mill (known then as the Cricketers Mill) as their Clubhouse. In 1895 the course was extended to eighteen holes, and in 1906 moved to its present 'home' at the AntiMill. The course as we know it today (with minor alterations) has existed since 1945, after the end of the Second World War. The Anti Mill Clubhouse has remained the responsibility of the Club and has undergone many changes. In 2018/19 the Mill underwent a substantial external and internal renovation, thanks to a grant from a local fund for Community Recreation.

In 1989 the Club celebrated its Centenary - it is arguably the oldest inland golf course in Yorkshire. Among many other celebrations at that time a delightful little treatise called 'One Hundred Years of Golf on Westwood' was produced, and we acknowledge this as the source of much information. The club continues to thrive and now has 512 members.

The course is a tribute to a dedicated band of groundstaff, and remains a firm favourite of golfers from near and far with its unique combination of uphill and down dale, wired off greens and, in the summer months, the ever present herd of cows.

62

BEVERLEY and EAST RIDING GOLF CLUB

Some love it some hate it,
But whatever they say
The golf course at Beverley
Is a pleasure to play.

There's cows in the summer
There's clap on the ground,
The greens are all wired
But they don't seem to mind.

The clubhouse was Black Mill
In ages gone bye,
But now at the Antimill
Our future does lie.

Uphill and downhill,
A cow in the way,
The rough can be devilish
The greens fast, they say.

There's Wentworth and Pebble,
Augusta and Troon,
St Andrews and Lytham
'Cos golf's on a boom.

There's Hessle and Hornsea,
Kirkella and Brough,
Maybe Ganton's the star
Much sand and deep rough.

But here on the Westwood
We're happy to play.
There's nowhere quite like it -
A halcyon way.

THE RACECOURSE

Records exist that date horse racing on Westwood from the 1690's, probably around 'The Tan Gallops', but it is likely informal racing took place long before then. Racing on The Hurn started in 1712 with Robert Norton, then the landlord of the Rose and Crown, being the first Clerk of the Course. In 1767 funding was started for the first grandstand with an issue of 300 special silver admission tickets. An annual meeting was established in the same year. Many improvements have taken place over the years including the building of the Tattersall Enclosure in 1968. In 2018 the proposed building of a new grandstand was announced at a projected cost of 4.8 million pounds. The course itself is described as right handed, one mile three furlongs in length, mainly flat with tight turns and an uphill finish. The Hilary Needler Filles' Trophy Conditions Stakes in May and the Beverley Bullet sprint in August are perhaps the most prestigious races. Under the guidance and leadership of Charles Maxsted and Sally Igguiden the Racecourse has continued to prosper, with 19 meetings taking place in 2018 including the famous Ladies Day.

The success of the Racecourse over the years has encouraged local trainers – one thinks of Geoff Toff in the stables behind The Royal Standard, W.H. 'Snowy' Gray and Alf Smith on Pasture Terrace.

If only for the names, look in Hansard, the Parliamentary records for 22nd June 1936, and you will see the East Hull MP, one Mr. Muff, complaining about the Beverley Racecourse Company encroaching on common land and his arguments being refuted by the secretary of the Ministry of Agriculture, Mr. Ramsbotham.

For many families of Beverley and beyond, the lasting memories of the racecourse are picnics in the inner enclosure on raceways - entry by car one pound for all the family (maybe slightly more now!) What a way to go racing.

AT THE RACES

It is two hundred years since they held the first meeting
High up on the Westwood, no stands and no seating.
But they thought as a site, it would take some beating
And that the idea was well worth repeating.

From the trainers, the riders and the bookmakers too
Who found a good living, they deserved a thank you.
Whilst the fee paying public found something to do,
Though the losers were legion and the winners were few.

But no one imagined we would see the day,
When the world of high fashion would go on display
At the annual fiesta that's called Ladies Day,
When the bars all run dry. Really, what can one say?

THE PASTURE MASTERS and THE NEATHERDS

Perhaps a little explanation is necessary - for visitors and even those of us who have lived here for years!

Freeman of Beverley: Prior to 2010 to be a freeman one had to be the son of a freeman, over 21 years of age, and born in Beverley when the parent was a freeman. It was also possible to qualify to be a freeman by servitude (i.e. apprenticed to a freeman in Beverley for 5-10 yrs). The Local Democracy, Economic Development and Construction Act of 2010 changed the 'rules'. The son or daughter of a freeman can now be admitted even if not born or living in Beverley. Part of the reason for the change was that the NHS, in their wisdom, had closed the Westwood Maternity unit and with the demise of home deliveries it was pretty difficult to meet the criteria!

A **Pasture Freeman** is a freeman of Beverley who lives within the boundaries of Beverley, Molescroft or Woodmansey. They are permitted to stock the common pastures of Westwood, Figham and Swinemoor. If they do not stock the pastures they are called non-stockers and receive money in lieu.

Pasture Master of Beverley: In 1836, an Act of Parliament awarded the management of the Common Pastures of Beverley to twelve Pasture Masters, elected annually from among the Pasture Freemen. Elections, to this day, take place on the 1st March each year, presided over by the Town Mayor. The Pasture Masters are responsible for the general management of the pastures, collecting rent called compensation from the racecourse, golf club and the hamburger van, collecting the 'head' money from the gaits, making, changing and enforcing the bye-laws, and for appointing neatherds (pronounced 'netherds') who are responsible for the day to day work on the land.

Each year the Pasture Masters decide how many animals will be allowed to graze on the commons. The allocations are called 'gaits'. One gait can be one cow, one horse, or 3 sheep and its lambs. Priority in the allocation is given to Pasture Freemen or their widows. At one time the **Neatherds** lived free in the six gothic style gatehouses built on the edge of the Commons. Now four of the gatehouses remain, one at the top of Westwood Road, one at the town end of York Road (recently refurbished) opposite the neatherds yard (Pinfold), one on Walkington Road opposite the Whiting works and one in Swinemoor. For many years Neatherd Jim Cornfoot was my neighbour – a familiar sight to all of us in his green tractor, accompanied by his sheep dog, controlling the unruly cows with great skill and calm. Now after 800 years we have the first female neatherd, Zowie Bell, whose job it is to tour the Westwood twice a day, examine the stock, maintain the pasture and hedges, recover stray cattle and sheep and if she has any time left help out at Figham and Swinemoor! We wish her well.

FULL MOON ON A SNOWY WESTWOOD

70

THE PASTURE MASTERS

The management of common land
Has more to it than meets the eye,
There are bye laws to be understood
With which these masters must comply.

They have to set the numbers
Of cattle that may graze,
Each animal is called a 'Head'
To use the local phrase.

'Tis they who hire the Neatherds
Who look after all the beasts
Which have been known to go to town,
Well, wander down our streets.

They collect the compensations,
Which we might call the rent,
From the Golf Club and the Racecourse
And a travelling circus tent.

But more than that, yes more than that,
They guard those precious spaces
From all the pressures that our times
Put on such valued places.

They're steeped in the traditions
Of those who've gone before:
The Westwood men, the Figham men
The men of old Swinemoor.

The Pasture Masters are local men,
They're Beverley born and bred.
They represent the status quo,
Although it must be said

They've had to make some changes
For progress don't stand still,
There's Pasture Ladies on the way
Born at Castle Hill.

WILLOW GROVE

The row of grey brick houses, several with hipped slate roofs, which face the easternmost end of the Westwood Pasture, were built in 1853 by M.L. Whitton with designs by his architect brother James Whitton of Lincoln. The grove gained its name from the row of willows or willow trees which had stood there alongside a stream which flowed from Westwood Pasture and fed into Walker Beck via the 'town ditch'. Previously it had been known as Willow Spring or Willowes Well. Very appropriate names, as the inhabitants of the houses in the floods of 1912, 2007 and 2012 will tell you!

In 2012 the houses avoided the devastating damage of 2007, largely thanks to the efforts and leadership of Les Diment, who marshalled the local 'troops' with sandbags and buckets, and kept day and night contact with the Humberside Fire and Rescue Services. The houses are now fronted by a red brick flood wall.

Within the Westwood Pasture Nerthherds yard (the Pinfold) is the million pound flood defence drainage system which was finished in 2013. Not yet truly 'tested', it will, hopefully, spare the inhabitants of Pasture Terrace, Willow Grove and beyond the trauma of the previous flood devastations.

74

WILLOW GROVE

On June twenty five two thousand and seven,
A day of Biblical weather.
Torrential rain again and again,
We thought it would last forever.

The water came over the Willow Grove wall,
And then, with an awesome menace,
It swept around with a swishing sound
And raced up Pasture Terrace.

Some idiot man in a big white van
Hit the waters unawares,
And caused them to pour right through our front door
And half way up the stairs.

Through the next few years, our hopes and fears
They bonded us all together.
As we set to work, it was our Dunkirk,
To thwart the bloody weather.

THE REASON WHY

The rhymes are done,
The paint is dry,
Perhaps you've glimpsed
The reason why
We love this place.

Its history,
Its handsome face,
Its busy streets,
Its open space.

And when at sunset
You espy
The Minster towers
Against the sky,
You'll understand
The Reason Why.

SOURCES

1 North Bar
> Historical Beverley: Wikipedia
> A brief history of Beverley, Yorkshire: Tim Lambert, www.local histories.org/beverley/html
> The History of Beverley, East Yorkshire: Pamela Hopkins, 2nd ed.,2011, Blackthorn Press
> The buildings of England: Yorkshire: York and the East Riding; Pevsner N and Neave D ,2nd ed., 2001,Penguin Books,p321
> Beverlac or History and Antiquities of Beverley, George Poulson,vol.1, Scaum,1829
> Historic England: www.historicengland.org.uk/listing/the-list/list-entry/1162565

2 The Royal Standard
> A Toast of the Town:Paul Gibson, Kingston press and www.paul-gibson.com/pubs
> The Inn Places of Beverley :Pinfold and Higginson , Hull Press, 1988
> Kevin Wild [personal communication]

3 The Beverley Arms Hotel
> Beverley FM: beverleyfm.com/history/beverley-history-the-beverley-arms-hotel
> Hull Daily Mail: hulldailymail.co.uk/news July 20 2018
> Paul Gibson: www.paul-gibson.com/pubs-and-breweries
> Bowman Riley Architects: www.bowmanriley.com/projects/beverley-arms
> John Markham: The Beverley Arms-Story of a Hotel, Highgate Press 1986

4 St Marys Church
> Many thanks to Dr David Bowden for writing these notes

5 The White Horse Inn [Nellies]
> Paul Gibson's Hull and East Yorkshire History, www.paul-gibson.com/pubs
> Mike Higgingbottom: Interesting Times: www.mikehigginbottominterestingtimes.co.uk
> Pat Deans: www.eastriding.gov.uk/calmviews/Record Local History Collection
> Pamela Eldred: Nellie Collinson in Extraordinary Women of Beverley, Barbara English ,Ed, Beverley and District Civic Soc 2019

6 Saturday Market
British History on line. www.british-history.ac.uk/Yorkshire-a history of the County of Yorkshire East Riding/vol 6/the borough and libraries of beverley/markets and fairs
A brief History Of Beverley, Tim Lambert www.localhistories.org /beverley/html
The sound of East Yorkshire: Beverley FM : Saturday Market www.beverleyfm.com

7. Market Cross
Beverley Civic Society: information displayed on wall of The Grapes Public House
Patrick Baty: patrickbaty.co.uk/2013/03/29/market-cross-beverley-east-yorkshire/
Cabbages and Kings: A History of Saturday Market, 2014, Barbara English, Ann Bennett, Susan Neave, Beverley and District Civic Society and the Georgian Society of East Yorkshire
Philip Brown's Beverley,Ed J Markham,1989,Humberside Libraries and Arts

8. Wednesday Market
British History on line: Markets and Fairs: www.british-history.ac.uk-a history of County of Yorkshire
Beverley and District Civic Society: plaque
The History of Beverley: Pamela Hopkins: Blackthorne Press 2nd ed 2011
Paul Gibson's Hull and East Yorkshire History:Beverley Pubs ,www.paul-gibson.com/pubs –and-breweries

9. Shops in Wednesday Market
Duncan Jack [personal communication]
Mrs Josie Peck [personal communication]
Mr Peter Brinham and Staff [personal communication]
A Nation of Shopkeepers: Bill Evans and Andrew Lawson,Plexus, London,1981

10 Highgate
The History of Beverley: Pamela Hopkins: Blackthorne Press 2nd ed. 2011
The Buildings of England: Yorkshire: York and the East Riding :Pevsner N. and Neave D., 2nd ed. 2001,Penguin Books p 312
Colin Bradshaw : Highgate : U3A local history group,Beverley, 25/04/2018

11 The East Riding Theatre
'By gone Beverley' in association with East Riding Archives 'Baptist Building Lives On'
Brief Notes on the History of theatre in Beverley : Susan Neave, 2014
East Riding Theatre [former Baptist chapel] documentary history of the site : Susan Neave ,2014
Documents recording the foundation and development of ERT [property of ERT]
Personal communication: Tom Wilders, Honorary Treasurer ERT, 2019

12. Beverley Minster
Beverley Minster: www.britainexpress.com/counties/Yorkshire/churches/Beverley-Minster htm
Beverley Minster -a miniguide : www.beverleyminster.org/visit-us-2/12139-2
personal communication: [anon]

14. Beverley Beck and Beckside
Pevsner and Neave Yorkshire: York and the East Riding p282 Penguin Books 2002
Beverley Beck Wikipedia www.wikipedia.org
Mediaeval Beverley: Trade and Industry British History Online: www.british -history.ac.uk
HU17.net Feb 5 2010: Iron Ship Building in Beverley U tube

15.Beverley Westwood Hospital
The Westwood Workhouse: www.workhouses.org.uk
Hull Daily Mail:15/12/2016
Westwood Hospital: British history on line
Westwood Hospital Beverley: www.historicengland.org.uk/sevices-skills/education/educational-images/westwood-hospital-beverley-8166
Westwood Hospital Beverley; www.historic England TA0275239476
HU17.net www.hu17net/tag /beverley-westwood -hospital

16 Westwood with Hurn
Westwood Common, Beverley. An Archeological Survey A1/25/2004
The History of Beverley East Yorkshire : Pamela Hopkins .Blackthorn Press, 2nd Ed.,2011
History Of Westwood and Beverley Commons: Helen Kitson.Nov 2018 www.U3asites.org.uk/beverley/20-historyofwestwoodandbeverleycommons

17 Westwood with Hurn Map
Westwood Common, Beverley. An Archeological Survey A1/25/2004

18. Westwood Mills
The History of Beverley, East Yorkshire : Pamela Hopkins Blackthorne Press ,2nd Ed ,2011
One Hundred Years of Golf on Westwood,Coxtons Publications,1990
History of Westwood www.u3a sites.org.uk
British History: www.british-history.ac.uk/ych/yorks/east/vol6/pp211-18

19. Beverley and East Riding Golf Club
One Hundred Years of Golf on Westwood ed JMG Ward Publishers Coxton Publications,1990.
[with permission Beverley and East Riding Golf Club]
British History on line: www.british-history.ac.uk/vch/yorks/east/vol6/pp211-218Hull and East Yorkshire News 1st Feb 2018

20. Beverley Racecourse
Beverley Racecourse: www.enwikipedia.org/wiki/Beverley-Racecourse
New grandstand: hulldailymail.co.uk/news/hull-east-yorkshire/news/huge-48mtransfusion-plans-beverley-1917655
Hansard: www.api.parliament.uk/historic-hansard/beverley-racecorse-company-pasture-of
Horse Racing in Beverley and Yorkshire: Ken Brooke, 2016, Blackface,Hull

21. Willow Grove
Complete Streets of Beverley, David Sherwood,p118 ERY Council Library 2002
Yorkshire: York and the East Riding Pevsner and Neave p 321
Mark Ewen [of Mott MacDonald Bentley] Presentation at WaPUG Spring Conference,2012
www.hu17/2013/09/19flood-risk-reduced-for-dozens-of –properties-in-beverley

22 The Pasture Masters and the Neatherds
History of Westwood and Beverley Commons U3a History Talk ,2018. H.Kitson
East Riding County Council: www.eastriding.gov.uk/council/civic-services
The History of Beverley East Yorkshire : Pamela Hopkins .Blackthorn Press, 2nd Ed.,2011
Hull Daily Mail: www.hulldailymail.co.uk/news/hull-and-east-yorkshire-news/who-looks-after-beverley-pasture
Agricultural Management of Common Land,Appendix1:randd.defra.gov.uk/Document-aspx?Document=LEO218_2565_FRA.pdf
Beverley Pastures Bye –laws 2004

DISCLAIMER: Every attempt has been made to trace and acknowledge copyright of material used in this book.
The publisher and authors apologise for any accidental infringements and would welcome information to redress the situation.